ideals®
CHRISTMAS

Vol. 50, No. 8

D1308782

Publisher, Patricia A. Pingry
Editor, Tim Hamling
Art Director, Patrick McRae
Contributing Editors, Lansing Christman, Deana Deck, Russ Flint, Pamela Kennedy, Heidi King, Nancy Skarmeas
Editorial Assistant, Laura Matter

ISBN 0-8249-1113-X

IDEALS—Vol. 50, No. 8 December MCMXCIII IDEALS (ISSN 0019-137X) is published eight times a year: February, March, May, June, August, September, November, December by IDEALS PUBLICATIONS INCORPORATED, 565 Marriott Drive, Nashville, TN 37214. Second-class postage paid at Nashville, Tennessee and additional mailing offices. Copyright © MCMXCIII by IDEALS PUBLICATIONS INCORPORATED. POSTMASTER: Send address changes to Ideals, PO Box 148000, Nashville, TN 37214-8000. All rights reserved. Title IDEALS registered U.S. Patent Office.

SINGLE ISSUE—$4.95
ONE-YEAR SUBSCRIPTION—eight consecutive issues as published—$19.95
TWO-YEAR SUBSCRIPTION—sixteen consecutive issues as published—$35.95
Outside U.S.A., add $6.00 per subscription year for postage and handling.

ACKNOWLEDGMENTS

CHRISTMAS COMES BUT ONCE A YEAR by Edgar A. Guest from *THE FRIENDLY WAY*, copyright © 1931 by The Reilly & Lee Co. Used by permission of the author's estate. SIGNS OF CHRISTMAS by Edwin Lees from *OUR HOLIDAYS IN POETRY* compiled by Mildred P. Harrington and Josephine H. Thomas. Published in 1929 by The H.W. Wilson Company. WINTER IN THE COUNTRY from *AGAINST ALL TIME* by Isla Paschal Richardson. Permission by BRANDEN PUBLISHING Boston. Our Sincere Thanks to the following authors whom we were unable to contact: Claire Mitchell for PURE WHITE WORLD and Florence Howery Roddy for DECEMBER.

Four-color separations by Precision Color Graphics Ltd., New Berlin, Wisconsin.

Printing by The Banta Company, Menasha, Wisconsin. Printed on Weyerhauser Husky.

The paper used in this publication meets the minimum requirements of American National Standard for Information Sciences—Permanence of Paper for Printed Library Materials, ANSI Z39.48-1984.

Unsolicited manuscripts will not be returned without a self-addressed stamped envelope.

Cover Photo
Fred Dole
New England Stock Photo

Inside Covers
Jay Killian

Pure White World

Claire Mitchell

There's a brand new world outside my door,
A world I've never seen before,
A pure white world no foot has trod,
A world that still belongs to God,

A reverent world, where even trees
Are offering prayers on bended knees,
Their heads bowed low, til sun's caress
Shall bid them rise, His name to bless.

This virgin world before me lies
To make my own through loving eyes;
I drink it deep, so deep, and then
I give it back to God again.

Photo Opposite
WINTERED BRIDGE
Near Parfreyville, Wisconsin
Ken Dequaine Photography

Winter
in the
Country

Isla Paschal Richardson

The sound of distant sleigh bells heard,
Sparkling snow upon the ground.
Wintertime! The very word
Has a pleasant, cozy sound.

Youngsters on toboggan sleds
Sliding down an icy hill,
Woolen caps upon their heads,
Laughter ringing, gay and shrill.

Merrily the back logs blaze,
Roasting chestnuts, popping corn.
Do you recall the winter days
On the farm where you were born?

Winter in the city? No—
No one knows its dazzling charm
Unless they've seen untrodden snow
On the fields around a farm.

The Snow-Storm

Ralph Waldo Emerson

Announced by all the trumpets of the sky,
Arrives the snow, and, driving o'er the fields,
Seems nowhere to alight: the whited air
Hides hills and woods, the river, and the heaven,
And veils the farmhouse at the garden's end.
The sled and traveler stopped, the courier's feet
Delayed, all friends shut out, the housemates sit
Around the radiant fireplace, enclosed
In a tumultuous privacy of storm.

Come see the north wind's masonry!
Out of an unseen quarry evermore
Furnished with tile, the fierce artificer
Curves his white bastions with projected roof
Round every windward stake, or tree, or door.
Speeding, the myriad-handed, his wild work
So fanciful, so savage, naught cares he
For number or proportion. Mockingly,
On coop or kennel he hangs Parian wreaths;
A swan-like form invests the hidden thorn;
Fills up the farmer's lane from wall to wall,
Maugre the farmer's sighs; and at the gate
A tapering turret overtops the work.
And when his hours are numbered, and the world
Is all his own, retiring, as he were not,
Leaves, when the sun appears, astonished art
To mimic in slow structures, stone by stone,
Built in an age, the mad wind's night work,
The frolic architecture of the snow.

Winter Fancies

James Whitcomb Riley

Winter without and warmth within,
The winds may shout and the storm begin,
The snows may pack at the windowpane,
And the skies grow black, and the sun remain
Hidden away the livelong day;
But here, in here, is the warmth of May!

Swoop your spitefullest up the flue,
Wild Winds, do! What in the world do I care for you?
O delightfullest weather of all, howl and squall,
And shake the trees till the last leaves fall!

The joy one feels in an easy chair,
Cocking his heels in the dancing air
That wreaths the rim of a roaring stove,
Whose heat loves better than hearts can love,
Will not permit the coldest day to drive away
The fire in his blood and the bliss of it.

Then blow, Winds, blow! and rave and shriek,
And snarl and snow till your breath grows weak,
While here in my room I'm as snugly shut
As a glad little worm in the heart of a nut!

Photo Opposite
THE SEASON'S WARMTH
Jessie Walker Associates

DECEMBER

Florence Howery Roddy

Bright December, we salute you,
Hallowed month of all the year,
Filling hearts with love and gladness
With your gifts of hope and cheer.

Month of ending and beginning,
Wonders of the Christmastide,
Crystal snowflakes earthward drifting,
Dark scars of the old year hide.

Lighted tapers on an altar
Spreading hope o'er all the earth,
As your songs of adoration
Crown with love our Savior's birth.

Radiant star in dark sky glowing
Hangs low over David's town,
Where a babe laid in a manger
Wore a bright and haloed crown.

Bright December, we salute you,
As we near the old year's end;
Let your miracles of Christmas
Renew our faith and love again.

Photo Opposite
WINTER CHURCH
Cornwall, Connecticut
Michael Giannaccio
New England Stock Photo

THE CHRISTMAS TREES

Mary F. Butts

There's a stir among the trees;
There's a whisper in the breeze.
Little ice points clash and clink;
Little needles nod and wink.
Sturdy fir trees sway and sigh,
"Here am I! Here am I!"

"All the summer long I stood
In the silence of the woods.
Tall and tapering I grew;
What might happen well I knew.
For one day a little bird
Sang, and in the song I heard
Many things quite strange to me
Of Christmas and the Christmas tree.

"When the sun was hid from sight
In the darkness of the night,
When the wind with sudden fret
Pulled at my green coronet,
Staunch I stood and hid my fears,
Weeping silent fragrant tears,
Praying still that I might be
Fitted for a Christmas tree.

"Now here we stand on every hand!
In us a hoard of summer is stored.
Birds have flown over us,
Blue sky has covered us,
Soft winds have sung to us,
Blossoms have flung to us
Measureless sweetness.
Now in completeness we wait."

Photo Opposite
NATURE'S CHRISTMAS TREES
Near Parfreyville, Wisconsin
Ken Dequaine Photography

FROM MY
G·A·R·D·E·N
JOURNAL

Deana Deck

CHRISTMAS CACTUS, Barry L. Runk. Grant Heilman Photography.

The Christmas Cactus

In my opinion, there are only two truly reliable, easy-to-care-for, never-fail, flowering houseplants: the African violet and the Christmas cactus. As a team, they provide an entire year's supply of spirit-lifting indoor color.

Both plants are somewhat like stray kittens; they seem so grateful to be in off the streets that they make almost no demands of you. I know some people prefer plants that must be continually misted, repotted, and cajoled into blooming, but I do not share their preference. I like plants that can be purchased in full bloom and will last for years, producing a show of blooms on schedule, with minimal fuss, rather than losing their blossoms the minute you arrive home. In fact, I've found that the more you ignore a Christmas cac-

tus, the better it seems to grow.

The Christmas cactus was not a traditional holiday plant in my family; I had been out on my own for many years before I ever encountered one. Then, I made the discovery which everyone must make on his own since these plants do not have warning labels attached. Not all Christmas cacti are what they seem. (Here, they become more like stray puppies. What you see—cocker, poodle, retriever—is not always what you get!) Some are Christmas bloomers, but some bloom at Thanksgiving, and others wait until Easter.

Once you make this discovery, it's a simple matter to buy several plants and enjoy them in succession. With the proper mix, you will have nonstop blooms from late October until March or

14

April. The reason is simple. There are several distinct species of Christmas cacti, and all bloom at different times, although florists seldom differentiate between them when they are sold. Since all can be forced into bloom for the holidays, they are universally marketed as "Christmas cacti" when, in fact, only one is genetically programmed to bloom in midwinter.

As its name suggests, a Christmas cactus produces multitrumpeted, rosy red blooms on arched or drooping bright green branches just in time for Christmas. A group of them in rustic baskets looks lovely trailing across the top of a mantelpiece during the holidays. A single plant on a coffee table or buffet adds a festive, exotic touch to the Christmas decor and is a welcome alternative to a poinsettia.

The Christmas cactus's close cousin, the Thanksgiving cactus, blooms much earlier, and its bloom, borne on longer, narrower stem joints, can be either red or white. The third member of the family, the Easter cactus, blooms in spring, has branches that droop less, and bears upright or horizontal blossoms of scarlet, pink, and red.

All three varieties are easy to care for. The worst sin you can commit with any member of this family is overwatering. While they are blooming, they should be kept slightly moist, but once the blooms begin to drop, they take a short rest period and should be watered sparingly until their growth period. The best time to prune and repot a Christmas cactus is after blooming, as it enters its semi-dormant state.

These plants are often sold in tiny containers and will usually benefit from a move into a more spacious home, although it is best not to repot them too often. When repotting, use a container about one-third larger than the one the plant has been growing in and provide a rich, porous soil that drains quickly. These plants cannot stand in water. Commercial cactus soil mixes on the market are ideal for all three varieties.

When pruning a Christmas cactus, use small scissors or pruning shears to cut each stem back by about one-third. Avoid cutting all the way back to the main stem. When cutting, form a V-shaped cut leaving two points at the end of each cut leaf. These points will each soon produce tiny buds, and new leaf sections will appear on all the pruned ends, usually doubling the plant's capacity for blooms. As soon as these new leaf buds appear, resume a regular watering schedule and feed with flowering houseplant food once a month. The plants will thrive if moved to an outdoor location with bright but filtered light, such as a porch or covered patio.

In August, Christmas cacti need to be given a long rest. Reduce watering and leave the plant outdoors. Check the plant every few weeks to be sure the soil doesn't completely dry out, but water sparingly.

Like poinsettias, Christmas cacti need a conditioning period of cool temperatures and darkness in order to break the dormancy and produce flower buds. Fortunately, a Christmas cactus is not as demanding in terms of the number of hours of darkness and daylight needed to produce blooms, and you will not be enslaved by the plant as you can be by a poinsettia.

To induce blooming, leave your Christmas cactus outdoors as the days grow shorter and don't bring it indoors until the temperatures begin to fall into the low forties and high thirties at night. By then, the natural shortness of the days, combined with the gradually cooler temperatures, will have awakened the plant. It will probably have begun to show buds before you even bring it back in the house. At this point, return to a regular watering schedule and fertilize the plant every couple of weeks with a 15–30–15 flowering houseplant formula.

Another nice feature of the Christmas cactus and its cousins is their easy propagation. During the summer, tiny root hairs develop along the edges of some of the older, outer leaves. Snip these off as described above, dust the uncut end with rooting powder, and set the leaf into damp perlite or sand. A root system will soon develop, followed by a brand new plant. If you start several and pot them in festive containers, you can present each of your friends with a blooming Christmas cactus for the holidays.

Deana Deck lives in Nashville, Tennessee, where her garden column is a regular feature in The Tennessean.

The Christmas Tree

Samuel Francis Smith

In all this bright and pleasant land
    Of sunshine, dew, and flowers,
Has sprung to life no Christmas tree
    More fair than this of ours.

Up from the strengthening earth, no sap
    Flows out from stem to stem,
But beauty crowns each bending branch,
    A Christmas diadem.

No faded blossoms, drooping, hang;
    No withered twig is seen.
Love set, and love adorned, the tree;
    And love is ever green.

And every little leaflet clings
    Closely to every other,
Like nestling bird to nestling bird,
    Like child to loving mother.

Brought from the field where once it grew,
    Alive, without a root,
'Tis not a fruit tree, but it yields
    The most amazing fruit.

What would you find upon the tree?
    Cake, candy, book, or pistol?
Perhaps not all, but love, as dear
    As any love in Bristol.

Then welcome to the festal hall;
    Come to our Christmas tree;
Come where the branches drop their gifts,
    Like the blest gospel, free.

In all this bright and pleasant land
    Of sunshine, dew, and flowers,
Has sprung to life no Christmas tree
    More fair than this of ours.

Photo Opposite
THE VILLAGE CHRISTMAS TREE
Waterbury, Connecticut
Michael Giannaccio
New England Stock Photo

Handmade Heirloom

THE NATIVITY, an original scherenschnitte designed by Marilyn R. Diener, Wyomissing, PA, who is a participant in the annual Kutztown Folk Festival, Kutztown, PA.

The Art of Paper Cutting

Heidi King

Paper cutting has almost as many names as patterns. In Germany and Switzerland, paper cutting is called *scherenschnitte*, and in Holland, *knippen*. The Japanese refer to the art as *monkiri*, and the Chinese call it *chien-chih*.

The technique of paper cutting dates back almost two thousand years and has roots in both European and Oriental cultures. The art, however, most likely began in China, where paper was invented around 200 A.D.

In the fifth century, the Chinese first cut paper patterns for embroidery. The intricate design would be lightly affixed to a piece of fabric and then embroidered over with brightly colored silk and cotton threads. This method provided a working pattern and stabilized the fabric. Because the patterns were just as intricate as the embroidery, paper cutting soon grew into a folk art.

Those who mastered the craft cut creations for decorative, religious, and functional

18

purposes. Homes were decorated with paper lanterns and cutouts, and, during funerals, the deceased's most cherished belongings were reproduced with paper and burned in a ceremonial rite.

By the seventeenth century, the art form spread to Europe. Because paper was still quite costly, monasteries were one of the few places that could afford to use paper for decoration. The monks cut magnificently detailed patterns to decorate religious books. As a result, many of the paper cuttings were religious in nature.

As the cost of paper decreased, its artistic uses increased. Paper cutouts were used as stencils to decorate wall borders in churches and homes. These stenciled designs, oiled so they would not absorb paint, were placed on the wall's surface to be decorated and painted over. After the advent of the printing press, carpenters began to borrow paper designs mass-produced in books to cut veneers from wood for embellishing furniture. Swiss paper cutters used a style of paper cutting called *marques* to authenticate and personalize legal documents. The Germans created intricate cards as tokens of love for their valentines.

Just as the names and uses for paper cutting vary, so do its techniques. Some Chinese paper cutters use large scissors with short blades. The artist first cuts the detailed inside patterns and then cuts around the entire design with one cut. Another Chinese method involves simultaneous cuttings. The paper cutter works on the lid of a wooden box hardened with a special mixture of charcoal and fat and lightly dusted with a coat of flour to prevent the paper from sticking. The paper is stacked, sometimes fifty or sixty sheets high, sewn together, and cut through all its layers with awls and knives.

Still another process requires that the pattern and a piece of paper be moistened, stuck together, and held over a lamp. After the paper has dried, the pattern is carefully removed, and an image is left on the paper. The image is sewn to the top of a stack of colored papers, and the pattern is cut along the image.

In Europe, many Dutch artists use knives instead of scissors to make *schneiden*, or paper carvings. In Poland, one type of paper cutting requires the cutter to use sheep shears to create the intricate designs, a practice that originated when Russian invaders confiscated small scissors from farmers and peasants. The Polish simply improvised and continued to create ornate paper designs.

When immigrants brought the art to America, early settlers not only cut designs from the paper but also painted exquisite details on and around it. Some of the more popular examples of this style are frakturs, which are fancy ink drawings created to record a family tree. Once fashionable wedding gifts, these colorful, exquisite designs can be made by a novice with a steady hand. Purse puzzles were also favored in early America. Similar to frakturs, these folded puzzles were often presented as love tokens in eighteenth- and nineteenth-century America.

Modern paper cutting employs many of the techniques developed by early artisans. The tools needed have virtually remained the same— a sheet of paper and any pair of scissors with sharp blades will work nicely. Detailed cuttings can be used as Christmas ornaments, bookmarks, note cards, shelf linings, lanterns, and wall hangings. A crafter may choose to imitate traditional patterns from Oriental or European works or create a contemporary design that reflects his personality.

Heidi King, a free-lance writer and designer, lives in Tallahassee, Florida.

Holly & Pine

Margaret E. Sangster

When Christmas comes
    With mirth and cheer
To clasp the circlet of the year,
Then forth we go for holly and pine,
Our wreaths of evergreen to twine;
Then swift we trip across the snow
To find the gleaming mistletoe,
And straight and tall and branching free,
We haste to choose the Christmas tree.

When Christmas comes,
    For Mother and Kate,
All sorts of sweet surprises wait;
And little fingers thrill with joy
As pretty gifts their skill employ.
When Christmas comes,
    Each tries her best
To make it beautiful for the rest;
And no one thinks of selfish ease
But seeks his neighbor to serve and please.

When Christmas comes,
    There is none so poor
He will turn the beggar from his door.
When Christmas comes,
    The rich and great
Search out their brothers of low estate.

And the sleigh bells ring,
    The church bells chime,
The children sing in the merry time,
And smiles and greetings leap to lips
That long were set in grief's eclipse,
For angels of comfort come and go
Within the Yule Log's radiant glow.

When Christmas comes,
    I think again,
Heaven stoops to wish good will to men;
And God, who loves this earth of ours,
With love once more
    The whole earth dowers;
And the Babe who slept on Mary's knee
Once more brings peace to you and me.

And storms may beat,
    And the winds be wild,
But the lowly mother, the Holy Child,
As in the manger, charm us yet.
All strife and evil our souls forget,
And each believing worshipper
Brings gold and frankincense and myrrh,
And the tongues of hate
    Are hushed and dumb
When again the Christmas angels come.

Photo Opposite
TRIMMING THE HOUSE
Original painting by John Walter

Signs of Christmas

Edwin Lees

When on the barn's thatched roof is seen
The moss in tufts of liveliest green;
When Roger to the wood pile goes,
And, as he turns, his fingers blows;
When all around is cold and drear,
Be sure that Christmastide is near.

When up the garden walk in vain
We seek for Flora's lovely train;
When the sweet hawthorn bower is bare,
And bleak and cheerless is the air;
When all seems desolate around,
Christmas advances o'er the ground.

When Tom at eve comes home from plough
And brings the mistletoe's green bough,
With milk-white berries spotted o'er,
And shakes it the sly maids before,
Then hangs the trophy up on high,
Be sure that Christmastide is nigh.

When Hal, the woodman, in his clogs,
Bears home the huge, unwieldy logs,
That, hissing on the smouldering fire,
Flame out at last a quivering spire;
When in his hat the holly stands,
Old Christmas musters up his bands.

When clustered round the fire at night,
Old William talks of ghost and sprite,
And, as a distant outhouse gate
Slams by the wind, they fearful wait,
While some each shadowy nook explore,
Then Christmas pauses at the door.

When Dick comes shivering from the yard
And says the pond is frozen hard,
While from his hat, all white with snow,
The moisture, trickling, drops below,
While carols sound, the night to cheer,
Then Christmas and his train are here.

CHRISTMAS FLORAL DISPLAY
Lincoln Park Conservatory
Chicago, Illinois
Michael Shedlock Photography

COLLECTOR'S CORNER

Tim Hamling

From left to right: the MAILMAN, the CHIMNEY SWEEP, the TOY MAKER, and the HUNTER. Photograph by Robert Schwalb.

Nutcrackers

Two disparate reasons—practicality and craftsmanship—account for the great variety of nutcrackers available to interested collectors. Since the most basic function of the nutcracker is to remove a nut's hard outer shell, the most primitive nutcracker design of a mallet and a hard surface is usually the most effective; unfortunately, this style offers few opportunities for artisans to display their craftsmanship. A second type uses a screw to press the nut into a flat, hard surface. This style is often used for hand-held nutcrackers and offers more occasions for stylish designs. Figural nutcrackers—those shaped like a person and using a lever to crack the nut between the figure's jaws—combine the functional purpose of a nutcracker with fine craftsmanship and an artist's imagination to produce popular collectibles.

Nutcrackers date back several hundred years. Early screw and lever varieties were forged from metal or carved from boxwood, an extremely hard wood able to endure cracking shells. These early lever models were shaped like various figures, but the early screw varieties were relatively undecorated. Most of the decorating on the screw-top nutcrackers occurred on those forged from metal.

The popularity of nutcrackers surged in the late nineteenth century due to Tchaikovsky's famous ballet, *The Nutcracker,* which endeared the figural nutcracker to millions and firmly established its association with Christmas. Like the wooden nutcracker who is transformed into the ballet's handsome hero, nutcrackers became treasured elements in holiday displays.

As these figural nutcrackers increased in popularity, so did their production. Skilled woodcarvers in Switzerland, Austria, and, most notably, Germany, produced great quantities during the end of the nineteenth and beginning of the twentieth centuries. Carvers usually used walnut or fruitwood, not the more durable boxwood; consequently, finding undamaged nutcrackers from this period is difficult.

During this time, metal casting companies in the United States, England, and Germany produced brass and iron nutcrackers in a wide variety of shapes and figures. Prices for these antiques range from fifty to two hundred and fifty dollars; but factors such as unusual shapes, original paint,

and condition can affect the price. The wooden figural nutcrackers produced during this period now sell for one to two hundred dollars, but prices again vary depending on the figure's condition and any extra materials, such as jeweled eyes or miniature accessories, that may have been added to complete the figure's authenticity.

Nutcracker collectors, however, are not limited to purchasing antiques. Companies today, led by Steinbach in Germany, are using both machines and hand carving to produce endearing wooden figures as artistic as those made over one hundred years ago. These colorfully painted, well-detailed figures, however, are unlikely to be used for their original purpose; most collectors choose to display their nutcrackers on shelves to preserve their condition.

Steinbach's nutcrackers detail figures from both everyday life and world history. The Chopin nutcracker sits composing at a miniature piano, and the Christopher Columbus nutcracker stands with an anchor in hand over a globe of the world. These miniature details also appear in the figures from everyday life. The hunter stands proudly with his rifle slung over his shoulder and his binoculars hanging around his neck, and the chimney sweep, traditionally a German symbol of good luck, wears his black suit and top hat while he carries a ladder to climb to the rooftops. The variety of Steinbach nutcrackers is great, ranging from figures representing common occupations, such as farmers, millers, pharmicists, and cobblers, to cowboys, Santa Claus, and Uncle Sam.

The trademark bared teeth and grin of a Steinbach nutcracker is said to ward off evil and bring good fortune to its owner. Although it is difficult to measure how much good fortune these figures create, the happiness they bring can be measured by collectors' smiles, which are as wide as the grins of the figures they proudly display.

Ideals' Family Recipes

Favorite recipes from the *Ideals'* family of readers.

Editor's Note: If you would like us to consider your favorite recipe, please send a typed copy of the recipe along with your name and address to *Ideals* Magazine, ATTN: Recipes, P.O. Box 140300, Nashville, TN 37214-0300. We will pay $10 for each recipe used. Recipes cannot be returned.

OLD-FASHIONED SUGAR COOKIES

Preheat oven to 375°. In a large mixing bowl, combine 1 cup of butter or margarine, 1 cup of vegetable oil, 1 cup of granulated sugar, and 1 cup of powdered sugar; cream until light. Add 2 eggs and 1 teaspoon of vanilla; mix thoroughly. In a second mixing bowl, sift together 4 cups of flour, 1 teaspoon of baking soda, 1 teaspoon of cream of tartar, and 1 teaspoon of salt. Stir dry ingredients into sugar mixture; blend thoroughly.

Roll a teaspoon of soft dough into a ball. Roll ball in granulated sugar. Place dough on ungreased cookie sheet and press down with a glass tumbler dipped in granulated sugar. Bake about 11 minutes until edges begin to brown. Makes 8 dozen.

Margaret Pruemer
Teutopolis, Illinois

FROZEN CRANBERRY SALAD

In a large mixing bowl, combine one softened 8-ounce package of cream cheese, 2 tablespoons of sugar, and 2 tablespoons of salad dressing or mayonnaise; cream until light. Stir in one 15¼-ounce can of crushed pineapple with its juice, one 16-ounce can of whole berry cranberry sauce, and ½ cup of chopped pecans.

Prepare two envelopes of powdered whipped topping mix according to package directions. Fold whipped topping into mixture. Pour into a 9x13-inch baking dish and freeze overnight. Serve individual portions on lettuce leaves. Serves 8–10.

Mary Masten Kimmel
Surprise, Arizona

APPLESAUCE CAKE

Preheat oven to 325°. Grease and flour a bundt cake pan and set aside. In a mixing bowl, combine 1 cup of drained, chopped maraschino cherries, 1 cup of chopped dates, 1 cup of chopped walnuts, and ⅓ cup of flour. Mix well enough to coat fruit and nuts in flour; set aside. In a large mixing bowl, combine 1 cup of brown sugar and ½ cup of margarine; cream until light. Add 2 eggs, one at a time, beating well after each addition. Add ½ teaspoon of vanilla and mix thoroughly.

In a third mixing bowl, sift together 1⅔ cups of flour, 2 teaspoons of baking powder, 1½ teaspoons of baking soda, ½ teaspoon of cinnamon, ¼ teaspoon of nutmeg, and ⅛ teaspoon of ground cloves. Add dry ingredients, alternately with 1½ cups of chunky applesauce, to sugar mixture, beginning and ending with dry mixture. Beat just enough to mix well, but don't over beat. Add prepared fruit and flour mixture to batter and stir just enough to mix well. Pour into prepared pan and bake in oven for 50 minutes or until toothpick inserted into cake comes out clean.

Wanda Cogar
Ravenswood, West Virginia

'Tis Christmas

Garnett Ann Schultz

A bit of hope, a bit of love,
A tiny part of cheer,
A smile, a thought, an outstretched hand,
A dream, all soft and dear,
Some faith and warmth and happiness,
And then a touch of prayer,
A bit of music, laughter too,
Of each a goodly share;

A window bright, a glowing fire,
Some holly and some pine,
A heart that holds a tenderness,
A peace on earth sublime,
Tranquility and thoughtfulness,
A soul to seek a star,
A bit of each, and then we find
'Tis Christmas—near and far.

28

Country CHRONICLE

Lansing Christman

I do not mind that December opens the windows of the year to another wintertime. Despite the wind and cold, the rain and sleet and snow, December brings a spark of love and faith, for the Christmas season is then at hand.

I still find the joy and exuberance I knew as a child. Living in the country all these years has kept me close to the joy of the yuletide, the real meaning of Christmas, and the hope and trust that come to one whose faith is based on the birth of the Christchild in Bethlehem.

I carry in from the woods an evergreen that will stand in the corner of a room. I decorate the tree with sparkling ornaments of red, green, gold, silver, and blue. The colors gleam in the brilliance of a lighted room.

From the woods, I gather ground pine to add its green to the overall atmosphere of the season. From the swamps, I collect black alder twigs loaded with their clusters of brilliant red berries to be placed on the mantel over the fireplace and in small vases around the room.

The countryside is covered in a blanket of pristine white. It shines like diamonds in the winter sun and glows and sparkles when touched by the light of the stars high in the heavens.

Bells and carols spread love and joy and add to the true spirit of Christmastime. As the birds visit the feeders outside my door, I hear this holy season of love in the songs they sing.

I need no other gifts as long as I have my loving friendships and the beauty and songs around me. I meditate and dream, for the memories of many Christmastimes continue to point the way to the birth of our Savior who promised eternal life for those who believe—and so I believe.

The author of two published books, Lansing Christman has been contributing to Ideals *for over twenty years. Mr. Christman has also been published in several American, foreign, and braille anthologies. He lives in rural South Carolina.*

Photo Opposite
RURAL YULETIDE
Original painting by R.A. Johnson

DECEMBER

Harriet F. Blodgett

Oh! holly branch and mistletoe,
And Christmas chimes where'er we go,
And stockings pinned up in a row—
These are thy gifts, December!

And if the year has made thee old
And silvered all thy locks of gold,
Thy heart has never been acold
Or known a fading ember.

The whole world is a Christmas tree,
And stars its many candles be.
Oh! sing a carol joyfully,
The year's great feast in keeping!

For once, on a December night,
An angel held a candle bright
And led three wise men by its light
To where a child was sleeping.

Readers' Reflections

Editor's Note: Readers are invited to submit unpublished, original poetry for possible publication in future issues of *Ideals.* Please send copies only; manuscripts will not be returned. Writers receive $10 for each published submission. Send material to "Readers' Reflections," Ideals Publications Incorporated, P.O. Box 140300, Nashville, TN 37214-0300.

A Shepherd, I

That mystic tale—the Babe, the star,
Three wise men journeying from afar,
Joseph watching near his Child,
Pious Mary, sweet and mild,
Bending over pungent hay,
The makeshift bed where Jesus lay.
The angels sang, by manger low,
The Savior's praise so long ago.
Now, when I hear church bells ring,
His glory too, with joy, I sing,
Then bow my head, deep wonder feel.
I, with the lowly shepherds, kneel.

Sarah Brandon
Phoenix, Arizona

Snow Gift

Season's manna, softly twirling,
Lands upon my windowpane.
What a wonder forming yonder
As I view the wintery lane.
Magic artist, gently brushing,
Gives to me a silent show.
God-in-heaven's Christmas gift
Is falling in the form of snow.

Blaka Y. Abee
Connelly Springs, North Carolina

The Crèche

Come to the manger. Come and see
Our scene of the Nativity:
The little stable with no door,
A makeshift crib
On straw-strewn floor,
The newborn baby lying there
Attended by the holy pair,
The shepherds, meek,
The ass, the sheep,
The Magi with a quest to keep.

How long ago, and yet how near,
The shining star still draws us here.
Another time, another place,
Yet we, too, seek the holy grace
To find the path
The wise men trod
Which led them to the Son of God.
We kneel, transported, to receive
The Prince of Peace
On Christmas Eve!

Ethel Dietrich
Lewisville, Texas

**A**nd it came to pass in those days, that there went out a decree from Caesar Augustus, that all the world should be taxed.

And all went to be taxed, every one into his own city. And Joseph also went up from Galilee, out of the city of Nazareth, into Judea, unto the city of David, which is called Bethlehem; (because he was of the house and lineage of David:) To be taxed with Mary his espoused wife, being great with child.

And so it was, that, while they were there, the days were accomplished that she should be delivered.

Luke 2:1,3–6

**A**nd she brought forth her firstborn son, and wrapped him in swaddling clothes, and laid him in a manger; because there was no room for them in the inn.

Luke 2:7

O holy night! The stars are brightly shining;
It is the night of the dear Saviour's birth.
Long lay the world in sin and error pining,
Till he appeared and the soul felt its worth.
A thrill of hope, the weary world rejoices,
For yonder breaks a new and glorious morn!
Fall on your knees! O hear the angel voices!
O night divine! O night when Christ was born!
O night divine! O night, O night divine!

And there were in the same country shepherds abiding in the field, keeping watch over their flock by night. And, lo, the angel of the Lord came upon them, and the glory of the Lord shone round about them: and they were sore afraid. And the angel said unto them, Fear not: for, behold, I bring you good tidings of great joy, which shall be to all people. For unto you is born this day in the city of David a Saviour, which is Christ the Lord. And this shall be a sign unto you: Ye shall find the babe wrapped in swaddling clothes, lying in a manger. And suddenly there was with the angel a multitude of the heavenly host praising God, and saying, Glory to God in the highest, and on earth peace, good will toward men.

Luke 2:8–14

The first noel, the angel did say,
Was to certain poor shepherds in fields as they lay;
In fields where they lay keeping their sheep,
On a cold winter's night that was so deep.
Noel, Noel, Noel, Noel! Born is the King of Israel!

They looked up and saw a star
Shining in the East beyond them far;
And to the earth it gave great light,
And so it continued both day and night.
Noel, Noel, Noel, Noel! Born is the King of Israel!

Photo Opposite
THE ANGEL OF THE LORD
Original painting by Joseph Maniscalco

And it came to pass, as the angels were gone away from them into heaven, the shepherds said one to another, Let us now go even unto Bethlehem, and see this thing which is come to pass, which the Lord hath made known unto us. And they came with haste, and found Mary, and Joseph, and the babe lying in a manger.

Luke 2:15–16

Silent night, holy night; All is calm, all is bright.
Round yon Virgin Mother and Child,
Holy Infant so tender and mild,
Sleep in heavenly peace; sleep in heavenly peace.

Silent night, holy night; Shepherds quake at the sight.
Glories stream from heaven afar;
Heavenly hosts sing Alleluia;
Christ the Saviour is born; Christ the Saviour is born.

Silent night, holy night; Son of God, love's pure light;
Radiant beams from Thy holy face,
With the dawn of redeeming grace;
Jesus, Lord at Thy birth; Jesus, Lord at Thy birth.

Now when Jesus was born in Bethlehem of Judea in the days of Herod the king, behold, there came wise men from the east to Jerusalem, Saying, Where is he that is born King of the Jews? for we have seen his star in the east, and are come to worship him.

Then Herod, when he had privily called the wise men, enquired of them diligently what time the star appeared. And he sent them to Bethlehem, and said, Go and search diligently for the young child; and when ye have found him, bring me word again, that I may come and worship him also. When they had heard the king, they departed; and, lo, the star, which they saw in the east, went before them, till it came and stood over where the young child was. When they saw the star, they rejoiced with exceeding great joy.

Matthew 2:1–2, 7–10

We three kings of Orient are;
Bearing gifts we traverse afar,
Field and fountain,
Moor and mountain,
Following yonder star.
O star of wonder, star of night,
Star with royal beauty bright,
Westward leading, still proceeding,
Guide us to thy perfect light.

Photo Opposite
A STAR IN THE EAST
Original painting by Joseph Maniscalco

And when they were come into the house, they saw the young child with Mary his mother, and fell down, and worshipped him: and when they had opened their treasures, they presented unto him gifts; gold, and frankincense, and myrrh.

Matthew 2:11

O come, all ye faithful, joyful and triumphant,
O come ye, O come ye to Bethlehem.
Come and behold Him, born the King of angels.
O come, let us adore Him; O come, let us adore Him;
O come, let us adore Him, Christ, the Lord.

Sing, choir of angels, sing in exultation,
Sing, all ye citizens of heaven above!
Glory to God, all glory in the highest.
O come, let us adore Him; O come, let us adore Him;
O come, let us adore Him, Christ, the Lord.

Photo Opposite
THE GIFTS OF THE WISE MEN
Original painting by Joseph Maniscalco

nd when they were departed, behold, the angel of the Lord appeareth to Joseph in a dream, saying, Arise, and take the young child and his mother, and flee into Egypt, and be thou there until I bring thee word: for Herod will seek the young child to destroy him. When he arose, he took the young child and his mother by night, and departed into Egypt.

Matthew 2:13–14

Photo Opposite
THE FLIGHT INTO EGYPT
Original painting by Joseph Maniscalco

The Angel's Story

Adelaide A. Procter

Through the blue and frosty heavens,
Christmas stars were shining bright;
Glistening lamps throughout the city
Almost matched their gleaming light
While the winter snow was lying,
And the winter winds were sighing,
Long ago, one Christmas night.

While from every tower and steeple
Pealing bells were sounding clear—
Never with such tones of gladness
Save when Christmas time is near—
Many a one that night was merry
Who had toiled through all the year.

That night saw old wrongs forgiven;
Friends, long parted, reconciled;
Voices all unused to laughter;
Mournful eyes that rarely smiled;
Trembling hearts that feared the morrow,
From their anxious thoughts beguiled.

Rich and poor felt love and blessing
From the gracious season fall,
Joy and plenty in the cottage,
Peace and feasting in the hall,
And the voices of the children
Ringing clear above it all!

A Christmas Carol

Josiah Gilbert Holland

There's a song in the air! There's a star in the sky!
There's a mother's deep prayer and a baby's low cry!
And the star rains its fire while the beautiful sing,
For the manger of Bethlehem cradles a king.

There's a tumult of joy o'er the wonderful birth,
For the virgin's sweet boy is the Lord of the earth.
Ay! the star rains its fire and the beautiful sing,
For the manger of Bethlehem cradles a king.

In the light of that star lie the ages impearled;
And that song from afar has swept over the world.
Every hearth is aflame, and the beautiful sing
In the homes of the nations that Jesus is King.

We rejoice in the light, and we echo the song
That comes down through the night
From the heavenly throng.
Ay! we shout to the lovely evangel they bring,
And we greet in His cradle our Saviour and King.

Photo Opposite
WINTER LIGHTS
Chicago, Illinois
Michael Shedlock Photography

A Christmas Carol for Children

Martin Luther

Good news from heaven the angels bring;
Glad tidings to the earth they sing:
To us this day a child is given
To crown us with the joy of heaven.

This is the Christ, our God and Lord,
Who in all need shall aid afford.
He will Himself our Saviour be,
From sin and sorrow set us free.

To us that blessedness He brings,
Which from the Father's bounty springs,
That in the heavenly realm we may
With Him enjoy eternal day.

All hail, Thou noble Guest, this morn,
Whose love did not the sinner scorn!
In my distress Thou cam'st to me;
What thanks shall I return to Thee?

Were earth a thousand times as fair,
Beset with gold and jewels rare,
She yet were far too poor to be
A narrow cradle, Lord, for Thee.

Ah, dearest Jesus, Holy Child!
Make Thee a bed, soft, undefiled,
Within my heart, that it may be
A quiet chamber kept for Thee.

Praise God upon His heavenly throne,
Who gave to us His only Son.
For this His hosts, on joyful wing,
A blest New Year of mercy sing.

THROUGH MY WINDOW

Pamela Kennedy

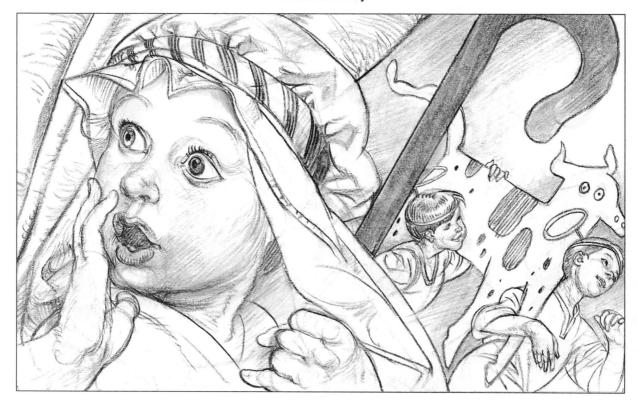

The Christmas Pageant

The idea of a Christmas play tiptoed into my head one day in early November. As I watched the neighborhood kids play in the tropical sunshine, I thought how these children of career naval officers missed so many of the community traditions of their more geographically stable peers. Wouldn't it be lovely, I mused, to create some special Christmas memories. When the kids trooped in for some snacks, I mentioned the idea of putting on a Christmas play in conjunction with the year's Christmas Eve service.

By the next day, budding actors and actresses had gathered on my front porch. Mothers were calling to ask if I had really offered to direct a Christmas play and, if so, how could they help. Any doubts I might have had about the popularity of drama in our small military housing area were quickly banished.

I decided to retell the traditional Christmas story, but chose to give it a different slant by dramatizing *The Innkeeper's Daughter*, a delightful tale written by a dear friend. Realizing the limitations of my time, talent pool, and theatrical experience, I opted for a heavily narrated script with few spoken parts and plenty of characters coming and going at appropriate times.

I offered parts to all the neighborhood kids aged two and older. Assuming the teenagers would rather be caught dead than in a Christmas play, I asked them to serve as "production assistants" in charge of creating the scenery. The preschoolers would be angels—an optimistic casting call. The elementary-school kids were the major players. Moms handled costumes and crowd control. Everyone really caught the spirit of the season, and the committees were humming along beautifully in the weeks before the production. From my perspective, things couldn't have been better. Then, we had the first rehearsal.

I realized something was wrong when the

leading "citizen of Bethlehem" wouldn't speak to the innkeeper's wife due to an argument over a boy at school. The angels had been entrusted to a college student home on vacation, who had drilled them faithfully in their choral offering of "Away in a Manger" only to find that half of them burst into tears when separated from their mothers. The two cows braced against the side of the packing-box stable resembled dover sole, each having two sad eyes on one side of its head. The mother in charge of the costumes was in a dither over how to make sixteen pairs of sequined angel wings, and a budding music student suggested that the singing would sound more angelic if it were accompanied by flute.

I eliminated the wings, suggesting halos would be sufficient, approved the flute accompaniment on a trial basis, allowed the angels to carry their teddy bears and blankets, and asked the teenagers to fix the eyes on the cows. We started a walk-through, and all went surprisingly well until Mary and Joseph were ushered into the manger scene by a grumpy innkeeper. Mary had decided to wear a pillow under her dress until the time of her delivery, when she went into labor, slumped to the floor, and brought forth her first-born from behind the manger to wails of "that's disgusting" from her beloved husband, Joseph, who then threatened to quit the play. The shepherds collapsed in laughter, and Mary, humiliated, fled the scene. We called a short break.

I found Mary outside and discussed with her the merits of illusion over realism, and we decided to forgo the pangs of childbirth. Joseph's mother had spoken to him, and the shepherds had been subdued by the time we returned. When the guardian angel finally marched her charges into the scene, one tripped over a shepherd's staff, and two more toppled over her. Their cries set off a chain reaction, and the whole group joined the uproar. The flutist interpreted this commotion as her cue and began a shaky rendition of "Away in a Manger." As we untangled weeping pre-schoolers, I noticed a group of mothers standing with their arms folded in critical appraisal in the back of the room. I began to think the pageant was a big mistake, but Christmas Eve was three days away, and I could not back out now.

On Christmas Eve, I arrived at the converted social hall an hour before the service. Someone had expertly touched up the animals; the cows wore serene, contented expressions as they watched over cardboard lambs and donkeys. Clean straw had been scattered around the manger, and a floodlight bathed the scene in a soft glow. Shepherds and citizens arrived wearing bathrobes, tunics, and sandals, and carrying wooden staffs. Pint-sized angels dressed in snowy tunics made of pillowcases gathered quietly around their guardian, who solemnly placed a glittering gold garland on each tiny head. Mary, Joseph, and the other players shushed one another as they gathered behind the scenery to await their cues.

After a hymn and a brief message from the chaplain, the play began. I sat on a stool at the corner of the stage and began the narration. In the darkened room, the awkward props looked almost artistic. Mary's delivery went smoothly, and Joseph even managed to look doting as the swaddled baby doll was laid tenderly in the manger. When the little band of angels trooped down the aisle, the only tears were in the eyes of proud parents. Like a silver thread, the tones of the flute wrapped around the players as the childish voices described "the little Lord Jesus asleep on the hay." When the story ended, there was a deep silence. Then, joyous applause burst forth. Bethlehemites, shepherds, and the holy family grinned with satisfaction. Parents claimed their young actors, and I overheard laughter as they recalled a special line or scene together; but my greatest satisfaction came as I heard a young girl tell her parents, "This is a night I won't ever forget." It seemed we had succeeded in making a Christmas memory after all.

Pamela Kennedy is a free-lance writer of short stories, articles, essays, and children's books. Wife of a naval officer and mother of three children, she has made her home on both U.S. coasts and in Hawaii and currently resides in Washington, D.C. She draws her material from her own experiences and memories, adding bits of her imagination to create a story or mood.

The Christmas Silence

Margaret Deland

Hushed are the pigeons cooing low
On dusty rafters of the loft;
And mild-eyed oxen, breathing soft,
Sleep on the fragrant hay below.

Dim shadows in the corner hide;
The glimmering lantern's rays are shed
Where one young lamb just lifts his head,
Then huddles 'gainst his mother's side.

Strange silence tingles in the air;
Through the half-open door a bar
Of light from one low-hanging star
Touches a baby's radiant hair.

No sound—the mother, kneeling, lays
Her cheek against the little face.
Oh human love! Oh heavenly grace!
'Tis yet in silence that she prays!

Ages of silence end tonight;
Then to the long-expectant earth
Glad angels come to greet His birth
In burst of music, love, and light!

BITS & PIECES

This is the month, and this the happy morn
Wherein the son of Heaven's eternal King,
Of wedded maid and virgin mother born,
Our great redemption from above did bring;
For so the holy sages once did sing,
    That he our deadly forfeit should release,
And with his Father work us a perpetual peace.

John Milton

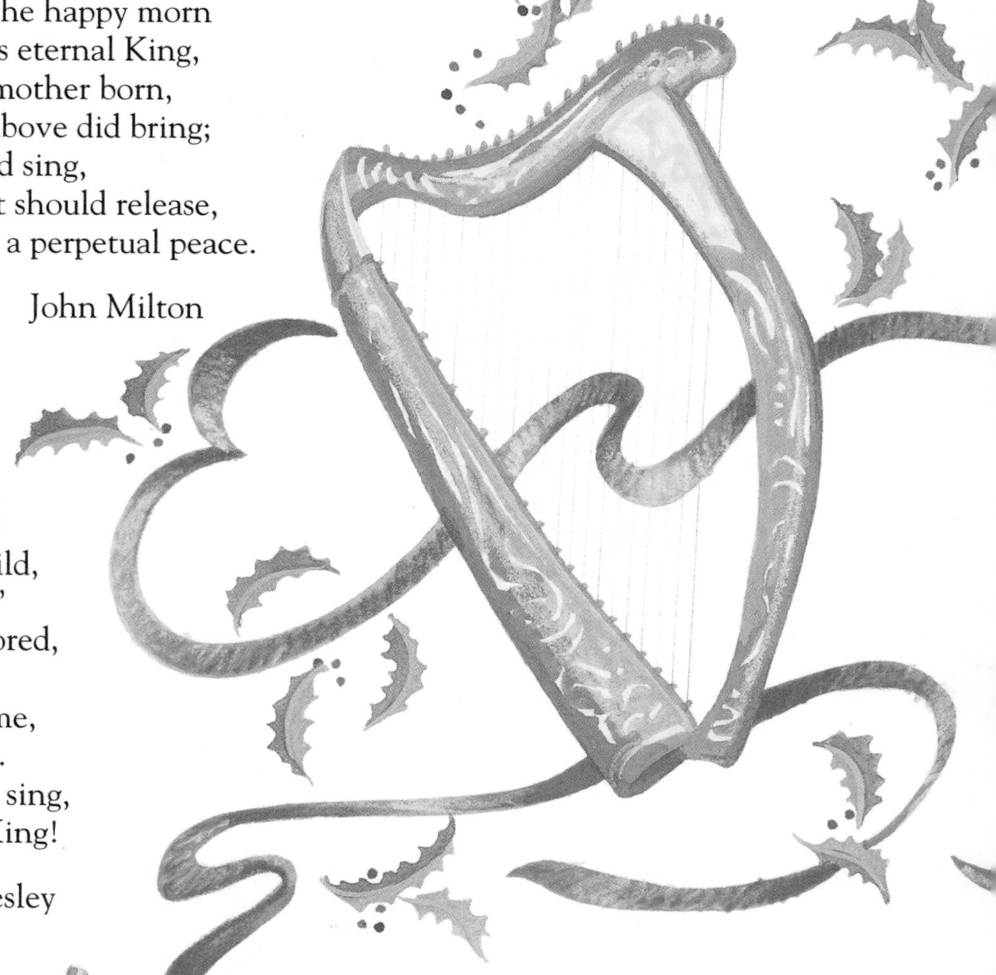

Hark! the herald angels sing,
"Glory to the newborn King!
Peace on earth and mercy mild,
God and sinners reconciled!"
Christ by highest heaven adored,
Christ, the everlasting Lord,
Late in time behold Him come,
Offspring of a Virgin's womb.
    Hark! the herald angels sing,
    Glory to the newborn King!

Charles Wesley

"What means this glory round our feet,"
    The Magi mused, "more bright than morn?"
And voices chanted, clear and sweet,
    "Today the Prince of Peace is born!"

"What means that star," the shepherds said,
    "That brightens through the rocky glen?"
And angels, answering overhead,
    Sang, "Peace on earth, goodwill to men!"

James Russell Lowell

60

Happy night and happy silence downward
    softly stealing,
  Softly stealing over land and sea,
Stars from golden censors swing a silent
    eager feeling
  Down on Judah, down on Galilee;
And all the wistful air, the earth and sky,
Listened, listened for the gladness of a cry.

            Edward Thring

Rise, happy morn; rise, holy morn;
  Draw forth the cheerful day from night:
  O Father, touch the east, and light
The light that shone when Hope was born.

         Alfred, Lord Tennyson

Good Christian men, rejoice
With heart and soul and voice!
Now ye hear of endless bliss:
     Joy! Joy!
Jesus Christ was born for this.
He hath oped the heavenly door,
And man is blest for evermore.
     Christ was born for this.

     John Mason Neale

The sky can still remember
  The earliest Christmas morn,
When in the cold December
  The Savior Christ was born;
And still in darkness clouded,
  And still in noonday light,
It feels its far depths crowded
  With angels fair and bright.
O never failing splendor!
  O never silent song!
Still keep the green earth tender,
  Still keep the gray earth strong;
Still keep the brave earth dreaming
  Of deeds that shall be done,
While children's lives come streaming
  Like sunbeams from the sun.

        Phillips Brooks

Ring the Bells

Lady Lindsay

Ring the bells, ring the bells,
Ring the merry Christmas bells,
And let their voice resound
Around, around,
Till o'er the leas and o'er the fells
The gladsome echo loudly tells
How we today are blithe and gay,
And how for all sad hearts we pray.

Ring the bells,
Ring the bells,
Ring the joyful Christmas bells!

Ring the bells, ring the bells,
Ring the merry Christmas bells.
So ring them high and low,
O'er ice and snow,
O'er cragged hills and silent dells
While round the earth the message swells
How we today are blithe and gay,
And how for all sad hearts we pray.

Ring the bells,
Ring the bells,
Ring the joyful Christmas bells!

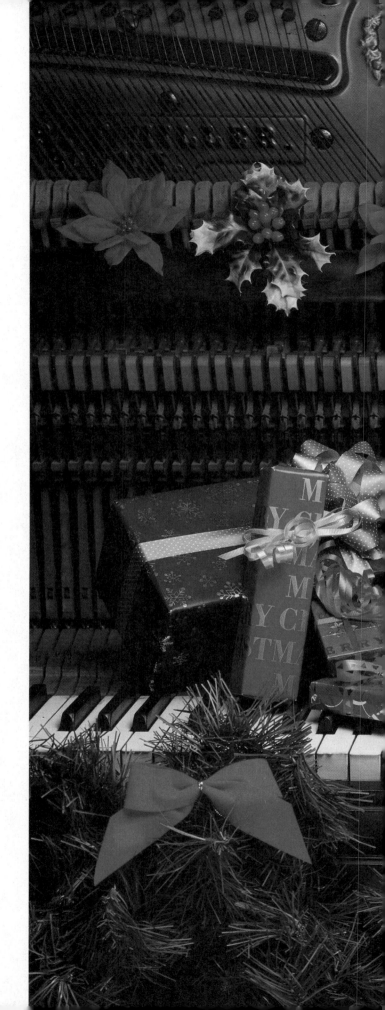

CHRISTMAS CAROLERS
William Johnson
Johnson's Photography

A SLICE OF LIFE

Edgar A. Guest

Christmas Comes but Once a Year

God grant ye joy this Christmas day;
    May every heart be jolly;
Love kiss ye now beneath the boughs
    Of mistletoe and holly.
The long, hard year of toil is done;
    Today the bells are ringing;
Put down your burdens every one
    And share the carol singing.

For Christmas comes but once a year,
    When harvesting is ended;
With merry din, the day comes in,
    By love and mirth attended.
The children dance and shout with glee,
    The eyes of all are beaming,
And high above the Christmas tree
    The Star of Hope is gleaming.

So homeward turn the car once more
    And give a kiss to mother;
Let horn and bell the glad news tell
    Of each returning brother.
For man has conquered time and space,
    Regardless of the weather,
And Christmas Day, by God's good grace,
    Should find us all together!

Edgar A. Guest began his illustrious career in 1895 at the age of fourteen when his work first appeared in the Detroit Free Press. *His column was syndicated in over 300 newspapers, and he became known as "The Poet of the People."*

Ann L Cummings

Tim Hamling

SECOND FLOOR LIVING HALL decorated for Christmas. Photograph courtesy of The Biltmore Estate.

Christmas at the Biltmore Estate

In 1888, George Vanderbilt visited Asheville, North Carolina, and became so captivated by the beauty of the Appalachian Mountain town that he chose it as the sight for his estate. He spent the next several years acquiring land and planning the estate's design, and by 1895, enough of the Biltmore House had been completed for Vanderbilt to invite family and friends to a Christmas Eve celebration. As novelist Edith Wharton described, the grand celebration combined Vanderbilt's opulence and his generosity:

Yesterday, we had a big Christmas fete for the 350 people on the estate—a tree 30 ft. high, Punch and Judy, conjuror, presents and 'refreshments.' . . . it was done so well and sympathetically, each person's wants being thought of, from mother to last baby.

Today, the Biltmore Estate continues the grand tradition established by George Vanderbilt with its magnificent Christmas celebration.

Many holiday traditions that today are an integral part of American Christmas celebrations—Christmas trees, poinsettias, caroling, gift giving, the image of Saint Nicholas—have roots in other countries. Vanderbilt had observed many of these holiday traditions in his world travels and incorporated them into his first Christmas Eve celebration. Today, these seasonal customs, traditions, and decorations from around the world continue to enliven the Biltmore Estate during Christmas.

The Pennsylvania Germans, who brought the tradition of the *tannenbaum* with them from Germany, likely inspired the thirty-foot tree that stood at Vanderbilt's first celebration. Today, in the same location, the Biltmore boasts a forty-foot Fraser fir tree decorated with brightly wrapped gifts and packages to commemorate Vanderbilt's generosity to the estate's children on Christmas Eve 1895. This first gift giving had its roots in the old-world customs, specifically in the Netherlands, the Vanderbilt family homeland, where St. Nicholas annually brings children their holiday gifts.

In addition to the giant Fraser fir, more than thirty other Christmas trees, each maintaining the decor and spirit of the estate's Victorian furnishings, decorate the Biltmore's rooms. In the Morning Salon, a favorite room of Mrs. Vanderbilt, is a "lady tree" appropriately decorated with lace gloves, parasols, dried flowers, and sachets. Other trees displaying candles, feathers, berries, glass and wax ornaments, lace, and ribbon complement their rooms equally well without straying from the original theme of the furnishings.

Holiday wreaths, garlands of evergreen, and poinsettias arranged throughout the Biltmore mingle their aromas with the scents of citrus, clove, and cinnamon emanating from the kitchen to create a unique holiday potpourri. Musicians and choral groups send the notes of favorite Christmas carols throughout the house.

On special candlelight evenings, five hundred luminaria light the front lawn, while fireplaces and globed candles illuminate the Biltmore's interior. Guided tours on these nights truly capture all the magnificent sights, sounds, and smells of the Christmas season. As the glowing flames reflect the holiday reds, greens, and golds and favorite carols echo softly through the halls, the grand spirit and festivity of George Vanderbilt's first Christmas celebration returns, preserving hundreds of years worth of holiday traditions by creating everlasting memories for each new guest.

THE BILTMORE HOUSE LIBRARY. Photograph courtesy of The Biltmore Estate.

Home for Christmas

Linda Heuring

Being home for Christmas isn't as much fun as coming home for Christmas. For nineteen of the last twenty-one years, I've traveled over lots of rivers and through dozens of woods to arrive home for the holidays.

Every few years, there was a car a little less likely to break down on the road, a new set of highways from which to view deer at daybreak, or a new speed trap to remind us that the police also worked in the wee hours of the morning.

I've brought a husband, a baby, and at least one dog, all settling into my parents' house for the long winter's nap on Christmas Eve. Santa found us there no matter what state was listed on our driver's licenses.

Our car was laden with baked goods and candy that were more expensive than those from any specialty store because the phone company, not the grocer, reaped the profits from my culinary attempts. The divinity took four long-distance calls to my mother, one of which resulted from invariably losing the recipe from one year to the next. I would call to find out whether I was supposed to use evaporated or condensed milk in the bonbons and again to find out the amount of peanut butter in the cookie recipe.

There were also calls to discuss presents when we were sure that certain parties were not listening in on the extension. There were the last-minute messages to let them know what time we were leaving, and there were calls en route if the weather was particularly bad and we knew they'd be worried.

With the help of a book light or the opened glove compartment, cross-stitched napkins were finished in the car on the drive—so were more than one afghan—but for the most part, the drive signaled the beginning of vacation. It was Christmas.

Bursting into my mother's kitchen while carrying a sleeping child or shepherding a barking dog, we'd see every available inch covered with her own holiday baking—the sugar cookies with sour cream icing, the divinity with nuts on top, the rum balls, and the buckeyes. We'd have to move containers of chocolate chip cookies to make room for the sandwiches she'd fix as someone's nonstop talking steamed up the windows.

We'd get our son to bed and keep my parents up way too late listening to music, catching up on the news, shaking presents, and eating.

Time was suspended. Work didn't exist. At home, I'd receive calls from the office, but here it was quiet. All calls were from cousins or brothers. Work was putting the decals on a fighter plane, untangling the controller wire on a video game, or opening my eyes after staying up all night with my brothers and their wives.

For the most part, Christmas was part of a time warp. Going home meant entering a twilight zone of sorts, a place where I could be a kid again, miles from my own house, my job, and my grown-up responsibilities. Oh sure, I packed the briefcase of work I couldn't leave behind, but I carried it up to my old room, where it remained until the trip back home.

Living near home for the first time as an adult has put a crimp in my Christmas. Just spending the day with my family isn't quite the same. I miss the anticipation of the trip. My nephews and niece won't have grown too much since I saw them last, and when the day's over, I won't be headed up the stairs to my old room to take a nap.

Oh, I guess I could take the long route to my parents' house, but even the long way is less than a mile. I suppose we could spend the night there, but it doesn't make sense to make all that extra work for my mom when our own beds are just blocks away.

I'm not sorry to be home, just sorry that I can't freeze time and make Christmas last a little longer before I have to go back to my side of town and become an adult again.

Photo Opposite
CHRISTMAS MORNING
Henry J. Hupp
Laatsch-Hupp Photography

LEGENDARY
AMERICANS

Nancy Skarmeas

Clement Clarke Moore

Santa Claus, as he has been known and loved by American children for over one hundred and fifty years, was the inadvertent invention of a scholarly gentleman from New York City, whose simple gift of holiday verse to his nine children painted the picture of "jolly old St. Nick" that has since become a cherished part of American Christmas tradition. That gentleman was Clement Clarke Moore, and the poem he wrote for his children was "A Visit from St. Nicholas," better known as "The Night Before Christmas."

Clement Moore was not in the habit of writing verse for children. Fluent in French, Italian, Greek, Latin, and Hebrew, Moore was a distinguished professor of Oriental and Greek literature who was known for his rather serious-minded writings on religion, literature, and education. He was also a man of great wealth who had earned a reputation as a generous public philanthropist. Nonetheless, with nine sons and daughters, no matter what public roles he played, Moore was first and foremost a father; and as he rode home to his family estate outside New York City by sleigh one snowy evening in late December 1822, he was thinking not of the classics of ancient Greece or questions of higher education, but of a simple poem to delight his children as they gathered around him by the fireplace on Christmas Eve.

The poem that would be known as "The Night Before Christmas" began with the legend of St. Nicholas, which had been part of Christmas lore throughout the world since 300 A.D., when the real St. Nicholas became known for his kindness and generosity with the children of Asia Minor. Throughout the centuries, the legend of the kindly saint evolved, with each culture adding its own details while absorbing him into its holiday traditions.

St. Nicholas came to America with the Dutch who settled New York, but he did not become American until that night in 1822 when Clement Clarke Moore made him the central character in his poem and fashioned for him a new, truly American, identity. Moore gave St. Nicholas his sleigh with its jingling bells, his "eight tiny reindeer" with the uncanny ability to fly up on rooftops, and his magical trick of sliding down chimneys to fill the children's stockings with gifts. Moore also gave the American Santa Claus a physical identity. Moore drew much of this identity from a sweet old Dutch man who worked on his family's estate. This unknowing Dutchman—a descendant of the very people who had first brought St. Nicholas to America—was the model for Santa Claus's white beard and fur-trimmed red coat. From this one unknowing Dutchman came the dimples and the rosy cheeks, the "droll little mouth" and the "little round belly, that shook when he laughed like a bowlful of jelly." With this now anonymous Dutchman, the age-old legend of St. Nicholas, and his own dear children for inspiration, Clement Moore painted a portrait of an American Santa Claus.

Of course, Moore had no such grand intentions that night. He wanted nothing more than the delight of his own children. In fact, Moore never sought publication for his poem; he never even wished to have it read outside his home, but "The Night Before Christmas" proved to be a classic with a life of its own. A meddling friend ignored Moore's wishes to keep his poem in the family and sent it anonymously to a newspaper in Troy, New York, where it was published just before Christmas 1823. From there it was out of Moore's hands. People copied the lines from the newspaper and read them to their own families and passed them on to friends. Within a few years, almost everyone in America had read Clement Moore's simple Christmas poem.

For almost a quarter of a century, Clement Moore refused to publicly acknowledge authorship of "The Night Before Christmas." He was surprised, and almost embarrassed, that his simple Christmas verse received so much attention. The poem, however, did not suffer from its years without an acknowledged author. It was a poem that every parent could claim as his or her own, and that every child could take delight in on Christmas Eve. From the day in 1823 when it first appeared in print, "The Night Before Christmas" became the property of every American child who shares the hopes and dreams of Christmas.

Clement Moore, inspired by his love for his own children, created a new American tradition. Today, we can imagine no other vision of our beloved Santa Claus than the white-bearded man with the rosy red cheeks and a red, fur-lined coat. And flying reindeer—why of course they fly! How else would they get up on the rooftops?

Old Christmas Returned

Old English Carol

All you that to feasting and mirth are inclined,
Come here is good news
   for to pleasure your mind.
Old Christmas is come for to keep open house;
He scorns to be guilty of starving a mouse.
Then come, boys, and welcome
   for diet the chief,
Plum pudding, goose, capon,
   minced pies, and roast beef.

The holly and ivy about the walls wind
And show that we ought
   to our neighbors be kind,
Inviting each other for pastime and sport;
And where we best fare, there we most do resort.
We fail not of victuals,
   and that of the chief,
Plum pudding, goose, capon,
   minced pies, and roast beef.

All travellers, as they do pass on their way,
At gentlemen's halls
   are invited to stay,
Themselves to refresh and their horses to rest,
Since that he must be Old Christmas's guest.
Nay, the poor shall not want,
   but have for relief,
Plum pudding, goose, capon,
   minced pies, and roast beef.

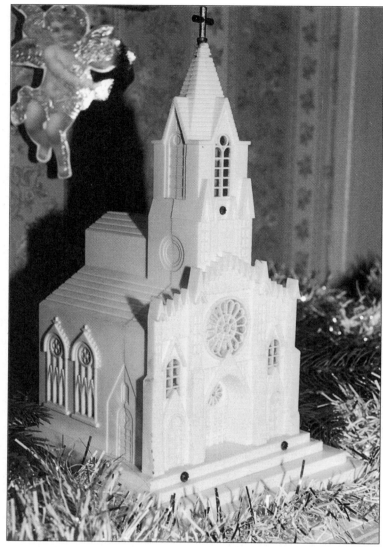

MOM'S CHRISTMAS MUSIC BOX. Photograph courtesy of the author.

Mom's Christmas Music Box

Brenda West

I carefully lifted the small box from the top shelf of the bedroom closet. Standing tiptoe on a dining-room chair, I stretched farther than gravity allowed and lurched forward. As I struggled to regain my balance, I envisioned a long-dreaded disaster.

"Oh no," I muttered, "after all these years, all I need to do now is drop this treasure. After all, it's an irreplaceable keepsake."

I managed to retain my composure and climb down, planting my feet firmly on the floor.

Shakily, I clutched the box in both hands and sank into the living-room recliner. After resting momentarily, I removed the lid from the cardboard container and pushed aside a mound of crumpled tissue paper. Nestled safely inside was a tiny, molded-plastic church, complete with a key-wound music box. Its original white color had turned to ivory over time, but the miniature had remained in almost perfect condition.

The small house of worship featured authentic detailing, from the steeple topped with a "gold" cross to the double-entrance doors and "stained-glass" windows. Four surrounding steps formed the base. I plugged in the detachable cord holding a clear glass bulb. Instantly, brilliant illumination flooded the interior and shone through the delicate windows, evoking serenity and reverence while creating varicolored hues.

I wound the key and placed the memento on the mantel. The tinkling sounds of "Silent Night" floated through the quiet house. Missy and Tuffy, my nonchalant cats, were quickly roused. Forgetting the intrusion on their naps, they padded toward me and stared intently at the new attraction. Eyeing the music box curiously, the two curled up beside my chair and purred contentedly.

When the last note faded, I twisted the key once more. Slowly, the present faded to mid-December 1952. Mom was supervising my two younger brothers and me as we trimmed our fresh-cut evergreen. The piquant scent of pine filled the rooms as it mingled with other pleasing aromas of homemade cakes, cookies, and candy. We three were bursting with pre-Christmas excitement, hoping Santa Claus would be generous on his visit to our house.

As we finished tossing tinsel on the tree, Mom's eyes gleamed and a secretive smile spread across her face. We watched in anticipation as she opened a newly delivered package from a mail-order house. As she took her time to cut the strings and remove the brown paper wrapping, we barely contained our mounting curiosity. With the aplomb of a skillful magician anxious to mesmerize his audience, Mom revealed her surprise— a church music box. Tenderly, she held up the small object, allowing us to inspect it from every angle. We were permitted to look but not touch.

My brothers and I squirmed in anticipation as Mom, clearly amused by our reaction, ceremoniously turned the key. Within our hushed circle, the first notes of "Silent Night" burst forth. We listened attentively until the last note quivered abruptly to an end. Then, we urged Mom to play it again . . . and again.

The evening passed quickly as we became enchanted by the sound and sight of Mom's music box. While we listened repeatedly to the familiar refrain, we could almost picture the manger scene being reenacted in the sanctuary before a hushed congregation.

How powerful is the childish imagination! Often, it is the cushion that softens the harsh blows of life. If only the elusive trait survived the transition to adulthood, perhaps we could retain our childlike wonder of the miracle of Christmas.

The church music box became a tradition at our home, filling a role as vital as the tree, lights, and other decorations; but as we rushed headlong into growing up, the music box, like the other decorations, grew less prominent until it was put away and nearly forgotten.

Somehow, the church escaped damage during its faithful service, including several moves to other houses. Recently, Mom relinquished the cherished possession to me because I had expressed a sentimental attachment to it.

Many Christmases have come and gone, yet the miniature church continues faithfully to ring forth the beloved carol. Its presence serves as a reminder of the Living Gift bestowed upon our troubled earth many centuries ago on a silent, starlit night.

That Gracious Gift offers peace and joy to all who will accept.

Carol

Kenneth Grahame

Villagers all, this frosty tide,
Let your doors swing open wide;
Though wind may follow, and snow beside,
Yet draw us in by your fire to bide.
Joy shall be yours in the morning!

Here we stand in the cold and the sleet,
Blowing fingers and stamping feet,
Come from far away you to greet,
You by the fire and we in the street,
Bidding you joy in the morning!

For ere one half of the night was gone,
Sudden a star has led us on,
Raining bliss and benison,
Bliss tomorrow and more anon,
Joy for every morning!

Goodman Joseph toiled through the snow,
Saw the star o'er a stable low;
Mary she might not further go,
Welcome thatch and litter below.
Joy was hers in the morning!

And then they heard the angels tell,
"Who were the first to cry 'Noel'?
Animals all, as it befell,
In the stable where they did dwell!
Joy shall be theirs in the morning!"

Photo Opposite
SING A JOYFUL SONG
Original painting by Ray App

"God Bless Us, Every One," Said Tiny Tim

I remember that Christmas morning three or four years ago when, with the utter abandon of the moment, we sat around the green-boughed tree whose essence permeated the whole room, unwrapping presents with shrieks of excitement as fast as hands could deal with tissue paper and tinsel knots. It should have been a moment of absolute bliss for all of us. But really, it wasn't.

It was almost what it should have been, but not quite; it somehow just missed the mark. It was excitement but oddly strained and hysterical, and the children had too many gifts and were suffering from acquisitive indigestion.

I wonder how many other middle-class American homes have known that little disappointed feeling right in the heart of Christmas? The feeling that something, somehow, has gone out of the mighty festival that should be there, and that something has unaccountably come in that was never intended? In a simpler day such things wouldn't occur.

Obviously something is wrong. Christmas isn't meant to be like this. It reminds me oddly of that lovely mysterious gift that Phyllis one year was sure she had received, the loveliest gift of all, but which she could never find, search where she would in all the debris and litter of tissue paper and gilt wrappings that were left about the tree.

What to do about it? One could be heroic, of course, and simply cut down the number of gifts to one or two, but think of the uproar that would start! Yet it was possible, as my family found, by less drastic means, to spread out and make the approach to Christmas a little different so that the worst pitfalls were avoided.

What we try to do is simply to spread the excitement over a somewhat longer period so that there will not be that sad mid-morning letdown when the last gift is unwrapped and we know that not till another Yuletide will the occasion come again; and second, by taking a pause now and then, to create circumstances that will invoke the larger meaning of the whole affair.

Try once more the magic of *A Christmas Carol*. If you don't have time for the whole thing, you can still get an amazing pick-up from two special passages. They are routine with our family; they take only five minutes or so to read aloud and are superb.

"Then up rose Mrs. Cratchit, Cratchit's wife, dressed out but poorly in a twice-turned gown. . . ." That is how it starts. It is in the next-to-the-last chapter, and it goes on, of course, about the Cratchit family's gorgeous celebration, and about that goose, the "feathered phenomenon," and the joy of Tiny Tim, who cried "God bless us, every one!" the last of all.

That passage for a page or so has to be read aloud every Christmas Eve in our family, and the children listen starry-eyed and the grown folks simply sigh and sop it up. Yes, we realize, that was what we were striving for all the time in those crowded, awful shops, that is what made it all worth while, and why we will do it again next Christmas. And the second passage is just as good, or better—the final pages about old Scrooge's redemption at his nephew's feast and how he bought the mighty turkey, and got dressed that morning in such a state of titillating joy that, says the author, "if he had cut the end of his nose off, he would have put a piece of sticking plaster over it and been quite satisfied."

AWAITING THE CHRISTMAS MIRACLE.

We have another final bit of reading, too; it is the last thing after the children have come down in their nightgowns and pajamas for a concluding look and good-night. I have to confess that this has a slightly ulterior purpose, too, otherwise we should never get them off to sleep. This is the brief passage covering the simple story of the birth of Jesus. After it is read, and after goodnights, the children troop upstairs, quiet, subdued, and happy for what is to come. They know it is the final event before Christmas itself. The excitement and tension have subtly altered. It is not merely a holiday lark any more after this reading, with a great acquisition of good things; it is something besides that. It is the mood of comfort and hope, the appeal of the Spirit that makes us all happier, and draws us closer together, and makes us more of one family. In fact, Dickens before bedtime helps to make the affair part of family love and affection everywhere, and this Bible story afterward links it with the spirit of God. As one very inconspicuous American parent, I recommend some such procedure as this as an antidote to the rather indefinite but very real problem of the modern Christmas.

Originally printed in The Christian Science Monitor, *December 18, 1943.*

Readers' Forum

The *Christmas Ideals 1952* was treasured by me as a young boy. My mother gave this issue to me, and I continued the tradition of reading it to my four daughters on Christmas Eve during their growing years. Their favorite stories were *The Night Before Christmas* and *Annie and Willie's Prayer.* I now have the pleasure of taking the issue from the shelf once again on Christmas Eve and reading the same stories to my granddaughter.

G. Robert Royer
Cape May, New Jersey

Editor's Note: This issue features Clement Clarke Moore, the author of the timeless Christmas classic, "The Night Before Christmas," on pages 70–71.

Just finished putting my Christmas books and magazines back on the shelf for another year.

I am 83½ years old and have quite a collection of Christmas books and *Ideals.*

During the Christmas season in 1948, one of my students gave me my first copy of *Christmas Ideals.* It was the second edition. I thought it was beautiful. There have been very few Christmases since without my new *Ideals.*

Juanita Clift
Bethany, Missouri

JOHN DRUCKENMILLER

ideals®
Celebrating Life's Most Treasured Moments